THE ULTIMATE
LOS ANGELES LAKERS
TRIVIA BOOK

A Collection of Amazing Trivia Quizzes
and Fun Facts for Die-Hard L.A. Lakers Fans!

Ray Walker

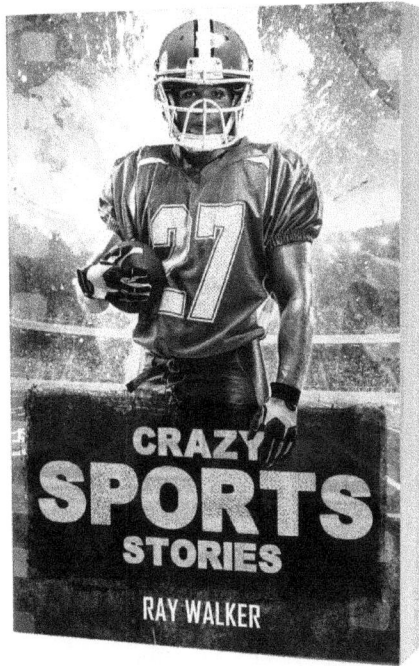

CONTENTS

INTRODUCTION

Team fandom should be inspirational. Our attachment to our favorite teams should fill us with pride, excitement, loyalty, and a sense of fulfillment in knowing that we are part of a community with many other fans who feel the same way.

Los Angeles Lakers fans are no exception. With a rich, successful history in the NBA, the Lakers have inspired their supporters to strive for greatness through their tradition of colorful players, memorable eras, big moves, and unique moments.

This book is meant to be a celebration of those moments and an examination of the interesting, impressive, or important details that allow us to understand the full stories behind the players and the team. Most of this book is focused on the team's time in Los Angeles, but the Lakers had an impressive tenure in Minneapolis as well and that is not ignored here. When thinking about your answers, read the question carefully; sometimes, it will refer strictly to Minneapolis or L.A., and sometimes, it will encompass the entire history of the franchise.

You may use the book as you wish. Each chapter contains 20

quiz questions in multiple-choice or true-false formats, an answer key (Don't worry, it's on a separate page!), and a section of 10 "Did You Know?" factoids about the team.

Some will use it to test themselves with the quiz questions. How much Los Angeles Lakers history did you really know? How many of the finer points can you remember? Some will use it competitively (Isn't that the heart of sports?), waging contests with friends and fellow devotees to see who can lay claim to being the biggest fan. Some will enjoy it as a learning experience, gaining insight to enrich their fandom and add color to their understanding of their favorite team. Still others may use it to teach, sharing the wonderful anecdotes inside to inspire a new generation of fans to hop aboard the Lakers bandwagon.

Whatever your purpose may be, we hope you enjoy delving into the amazing background of L.A. Lakers basketball!

Oh...and for the record, information and statistics in this book are current up to the end of the 2019-20 season. The Lakers will surely topple more records and win more awards as the seasons pass, so keep this in mind when you're watching the next game with your friends, and someone starts a conversation with "Did you know...?".

CHAPTER 1:

ORIGINS & HISTORY

QUIZ TIME!

1. In which year did the Lakers begin playing NBA basketball in the city of Los Angeles?

    a. 1950

    b. 1955

    c. 1960

    d. 1965

2. The franchise was nearly called the Los Angeles Lightning, partly to make use of the alliterative sound and partly because of the dangerous storms that frequently strike without warning in California.

    a. True

    b. False

3. How was the nickname "Lakers" chosen for the team?

    a. It was selected by the team owner Bob Short, who made his fortune as a ship-builder creating "lakers" for transporting cargo throughout the five Great Lakes.

b. It was chosen by fan vote, with "Lakers" (the common name for lake trout, the state fish of California) beating out "Lynx" (the state animal of California).

c. It was chosen by the team's founder, J. Sampson Laker, who also owned a Triple-A baseball team named after himself.

d. It was originally selected in Minnesota, which is known as "The Land of 10,000 Lakes," and then kept for the sake of tradition when the team moved to Los Angeles.

4. In which season did the Lakers begin to play in their new (and current) arena, the Staples Center?

   a. 1989
   b. 1999
   c. 2003
   d. 2009

5. Which person (or people) founded the Minneapolis Lakers?

   a. Bob Short
   b. Jerry Buss
   c. Ben Berger and Morris Chalfen
   d. Jack Kent Cooke and Bruce McNair

6. In which year did the Lakers earn their first division title ever?

   a. 1949
   b. 1954
   c. 1963
   d. 1971

7. The franchise was nearly sold and moved out of state to Kansas City in 1957 due to poor attendance, low revenue, and sagging interest in Minneapolis.

    a. True
    b. False

8. How many division titles have the Lakers won?

    a. 10
    b. 15
    c. 24
    d. 32

9. Which of the following players was NOT among the first three Lakers ever to be named as the team's representatives in the 1950-51 NBA All-Star Game?

    a. Center George Mikan
    b. Power forward Vern Mikkelsen
    c. Small forward Jim Pollard
    d. Point guard Slater Martin

10. Where do the Lakers rank among NBA franchises in winning Larry O'Brien Championship Trophies?

    a. 1st
    b. Tied for 1st with the Boston Celtics
    c. 3rd
    d. Tied for 2nd with the Chicago Bulls

11. How did the Lakers fare while celebrating their 50th anniversary season in the NBA in 1998-99?

    a. Lost in the Western Conference first round to the Portland Trailblazers

b. Lost in the Western Conference semifinals to the San Antonio Spurs

c. Lost in the Western Conference finals to the Houston Rockets

d. Lost in the NBA Finals to the Orlando Magic

12. The longest stretch the Lakers have gone without making the playoffs is six consecutive years, from 2014 through 2019.

a. True

b. False

13. Which team did the Lakers face in their very first NBA game in Los Angeles (which resulted in a 111-101 loss for the home team)?

a. New York Knicks

b. Cincinnati Royals

c. Philadelphia Warriors

d. St. Louis Hawks

14. Los Angeles's current top development team plays in the NBA G League. What is this team called?

a. Light City Lakers

b. South Bay Lakers

c. Hollywood Heroes

d. Cali Showtime

15. Which player poured in 34.8 points per game and finished as the team's top scorer in the first NBA season that the Lakers played in Los Angeles?

a. Point guard Jerry West

b. Shooting guard Gail Goodrich

c. Small forward Elgin Baylor

d. Center Wilt Chamberlain

16. As of 2020, Los Angeles is tied with the Boston Celtics and New York Knicks as the NBA franchises who have sent the most players to represent their countries in the Summer Olympics.

a. True

b. False

17. How did the Lakers fare in their first NBA playoff run after moving to Los Angeles?

a. Lost in the West Division finals against the St. Louis Hawks

b. Lost in the NBA Finals against the Boston Celtics

c. Won the NBA championship over the Boston Celtics

d. Lost in the Western Conference finals against the Detroit Pistons

18. The Lakers won their first officially recognized NBA title in 1949. However, the league was not known as the NBA. What was it called before taking the name we know today?

a. National Basketball League

b. Basketball Association of America

c. Professional Basketball League of America

d. American Basketball Federation

19. What is the official name of the L.A. Lakers' mascot?

    a. Louie Laker

    b. Captain Larry

    c. The Fighting Fisherman

    d. The Lakers do not have a mascot.

20. The Lakers spent over a decade in Minneapolis and several years in Los Angeles before taking up residency at The Forum, an arena they made quite famous.

    a. True

    b. False

QUIZ ANSWERS

1. C – 1960

2. B – False

3. D – It was originally selected in Minnesota, which is known as "The Land of 10,000 Lakes," and then kept for the sake of tradition when the team moved to Los Angeles.

4. B – 1999

5. C – Ben Berger and Morris Chalfen

6. D – 1971

7. A – True

8. C – 24

9. D – Point guard Slater Martin

10. B – Tied for 1st with the Boston Celtics

11. B – Lost in the Western Conference semifinals to the San Antonio Spurs

12. A – True

13. A – New York Knicks

14. B – South Bay Lakers

15. C – Small forward Elgin Baylor

16. B – False

17. A – Lost in the West Division finals against the St. Louis Hawks

18. B – Basketball Association of America

19. D – The Lakers do not have a mascot.

20. A – True

DID YOU KNOW?

1. When the Lakers were considering moving from Minneapolis to Los Angeles, the league's owners originally voted against the move, 7-1. With the threat of the team switching to a competing league and bringing the L.A. market to a competitor instead, the relocation was unanimously approved on a second vote.

2. The Lakers are not the only Los Angeles-based team to relocate to the city. The Los Angeles Clippers were originally the Buffalo Braves and then the San Diego Clippers before joining the Lakers in L.A.

3. Team owner Bob Short was heavily influenced when he saw the great financial success enjoyed by Major League Baseball's Los Angeles Dodgers after that team moved from Brooklyn. Short took the team from Minneapolis to Los Angeles, making them the first NBA franchise located on the West Coast.

4. While the Lakers are an anchor tenant of the Staples Center, it is not their home exclusively. They share it with the Los Angeles Clippers, the National Hockey League's Los Angeles Kings, and the WNBA's Los Angeles Sparks. In the past, their home has also housed the NBA D League's Los Angeles Defenders and the Arena Football League's Los Angeles Avengers.

5. When the Lakers are not in town, the Staples Center

configuration shrinks, losing about 800 seats, to host hockey, and expands by about 2,000 seats for boxing or wrestling. It is also used to house concerts for 8,000 to 13,000 people.

6. When Lakers founders Morris Chalfen and Ben Berger started the team in 1947, they did not begin from scratch but purchased the Detroit Gems of the National Basketball League for $15,000 and moved the operation to Minneapolis. No players were involved in the purchase; it was basically for the equipment and operation only.

7. Los Angeles's biggest NBA rival is generally thought to be the Boston Celtics because both teams have had multiple eras of sustained success, and they have faced each other in the NBA Finals 12 times. The Celtics have the advantage in the head-to-head rivalry, with a record of 161-131, leaving the Lakers with just a .449 winning percentage against them.

8. The Lakers and Celtics are tied for the title of most successful NBA franchise, with 17 championships apiece. Together, the two clubs have won 45.9% of all the NBA championships in history, and in many of those, they played each other in the final round.

9. The Lakers have an interesting history during their anniversary seasons. They made it to the NBA Finals and lost during their 10th, 20th, and 40th anniversary years. During their 60th anniversary season, the team won the NBA championship.

10. In the beginning, in Minneapolis, the Lakers dominated. The team won the NBA championship in its first two seasons and won three more titles in the next four years.

CHAPTER 2:

JERSEYS & NUMBERS

QUIZ TIME!

1. When they began playing in the NBA in 1947, the Lakers used what color scheme for both their home and away uniforms?

   a. Black, gold, and purple
   b. Red, white, and blue
   c. Powder blue and yellow
   d. White, powder blue, and royal blue

2. The numbers 0 and 00 have been banned from circulation by Los Angeles's ownership because they are seen to represent a losing attitude.

   a. True
   b. False

3. The number 22 has been retired by the Lakers in honor of two different players. Who are they?

   a. Forward Vern Mikkelsen and guard Gail Goodrich
   b. Forward Jim Pollard and center Kareem Abdul-Jabbar

    c. Guard Magic Johnson and forward Jamaal Wilkes

    d. Forward Elgin Baylor and guard Slater Martin

4. What did Lakers owner Jack Kent Cooke call the shade of purple he chose when switching away from the original color of Los Angeles's uniforms?

    a. "Royal violet"

    b. "Laker blood"

    c. "Majestic mauve"

    d. "Forum blue"

5. The number 34 has been retired by the Lakers in honor of which two players?

    a. Forward James Worthy and guard Jerry West

    b. Centers Shaquille O'Neal and Clyde Lovellette

    c. Guards Kobe Bryant and Gail Goodrich

    d. Center Kareem Abdul-Jabbar and forward Jim Pollard

6. Which jersey number has proven to be the most popular with the Lakers, having been worn by 25 players in Minneapolis and Los Angeles?

    a. 11

    b. 15

    c. 20

    d. 25

7. Lakers center Benoit Benjamin wore number 00 with Los Angeles in 1993. This was one of 14 seasons he wore the number, second most in NBA history to only Robert Parrish of the Boston Celtics.

a. True

b. False

8. Aside from George Mikan and his retired number 99, who is the player to wear the highest-numbered jersey in Lakers franchise history?

   a. Forward Dennis Rodman
   b. Center Markieff Morris
   c. Center Clyde Lovellette
   d. Swingman Frank Selvy

9. What unusual uniform issue did the Lakers experience continually during the 1980s?

   a. The team's players could not agree on whether to wear traditional short shorts or the newer, baggier style.
   b. The shades of purple did not match between their jerseys and their shorts.
   c. The jerseys were not breathable, leading to pools of sweat collecting inside and pouring out whenever the players untucked their jerseys.
   d. Players preferred a nearly identical unofficial replica jersey sold by street vendors outside the arena and attempted to wear these in games.

10. Center Dwight Howard is the only Laker ever to wear which of the following uniform numbers with the club?

    a. 69
    b. 59
    c. 49
    d. 39

11. Only one Lakers star was so impactful that he had not one but TWO numbers retired by the franchise. Which superstar was it?

    a. Guard Magic Johnson
    b. Center Kareem Abdul-Jabbar
    c. Guard Kobe Bryant
    d. Guard Jerry West

12. Star center George Mikan is the only Laker ever to have worn the number 99 and will always be the only one because his number has been retired in Los Angeles.

    a. True
    b. False

13. After Nike took over responsibility for creating the Lakers' jerseys in 2017, they introduced several styles. Which of the following is NOT a real style created by Nike?

    a. The white "Association" jersey worn for most home games
    b. The gold "Icon" jersey worn for many away games
    c. The purple "Royalty" jersey with black stripes in addition to gold and white trim
    d. The varying "City" jersey that pays homage to Lakers greats of the past

14. How many total jersey numbers has the franchise retired in honor of its former players?

    a. 8
    b. 10

c. 12

d. 14

15. Which player competed for the Lakers for just four seasons, the shortest tenure of any player whose number has been retired by the franchise?

    a. Center Clyde Lovellette
    b. Center Wilt Chamberlain
    c. Guard Slater Martin
    d. Forward Jamaal Wilkes

16. Twelve players have worn the number 1 for the Lakers, and every single one of them was a point guard.

    a. True
    b. False

17. Lucky number 7 has been worn by 17 Lakers players over the years. Which player wore it for the longest amount of time?

    a. Point guard Sam Jacobson
    b. Forward Lamar Odom
    c. Center Larry Nance Jr.
    d. Power forward Kenny Carr

18. Who is the only Lakers player to have a single-digit jersey number retired by the club?

    a. Guard Derek Fisher (number 2)
    b. Guard Byron Scott (number 4)
    c. Guard Kobe Bryant (number 8)
    d. Guard Nick Van Exel (number 9)

19. Which number did Verne Mikkelsen, who was one of the first three All-Stars named in Lakers history, wear on the back of his jersey in 1950-51 when he was first chosen for the game?

    a. 12
    b. 19
    c. 21
    d. 23

20. The Lakers have had seven players wear either 0 or 00, but have never had a season where two players wore these numbers at the same time.

    a. True
    b. False

QUIZ ANSWERS

1. C – Powder blue and yellow

2. B – False

3. D – Forward Elgin Baylor and guard Slater Martin

4. D – "Forum blue"

5. B – Centers Shaquille O'Neal and Clyde Lovellette

6. C – 20

7. A – True

8. C – Center Clyde Lovellette

9. B – The shades of purple did not match between their jerseys and their shorts.

10. D – 39

11. C – Guard Kobe Bryant

12. A – True

13. C – The purple "Royalty" jersey with black stripes in addition to gold and white trim

14. D – 14

15. A – Center Clyde Lovellette

16. B – False

17. B – Forward Lamar Odom

18. C – Guard Kobe Bryant (number 8)

19. B – 19

20. A – True

DID YOU KNOW?

1. During their time in Minneapolis, the Lakers just had wording on their jerseys with no logo. For the last few years of their time in the city before moving to Los Angeles, they displayed the word "LAKERS" surrounded by four small stars.

2. In the team's first incarnation in Minneapolis, the Lakers wore road jerseys that featured just the letters "MPLS" on the front. The abbreviation was used because the city name was too long to represent properly.

3. In 2016, the Lakers revealed Christmas Day uniforms that featured a V-neck and the words "Los Angeles" in scripted writing across the chest. While still using purple, the shade and the font paid tribute to the Los Angeles Dodgers' iconic baseball uniforms.

4. Some numbers have proven unpopular with Los Angeles players. Forty-five numbers have gone unused in franchise history, as no Laker has ever worn a jersey with any of the following numbers: 29, 36, 38, 46, 47, 48, 51, 56, 57, 58, 59, 60, 61, 62, 63, 64, 65, 67, 68, 69, 71, 72, 74, 75, 76, 77, 78, 79, 80, 81, 82, 83, 84, 85, 86, 87, 90, 91, 92, 93, 94, 95, 96, 97, or 98.

5. The Lakers have hung two banners in the rafters to honor non-players from their history. One reads "JK" in honor of Minneapolis coach John Kundla. The other says "Mic" and

is meant to retire the microphone used by legendary Lakers broadcaster Chick Hearn.

6. The Lakers' Christmas Day 2014 uniforms used a simplified version of their regular logo. They took the purple "L" from "Lakers" and superimposed it on a gold basketball to create a pleasant, streamlined look.

7. The number 13 was not an unlucky number for the Lakers. It was used by a handful of players during the Minneapolis years of the franchise. Only two players have worn it since the team relocated to Los Angeles, but because one of them was center Wilt Chamberlain, the number was retired in his honor.

8. Only one Laker has ever worn a jersey with a number higher than 52 for longer than three seasons before switching numbers or leaving the team. Hall of Fame center George Mikan wore number 99 for several years before the team retired it.

9. From 1960 through 1999, the Lakers used a block or shadowing effect to create the illusion that the numbers on their jerseys were three-dimensional. Since 2000, the team has usually used a flat, two-dimensional font with colored trim for their numbers instead.

10. Occasionally, the Lakers declare a home game at the Staples Center to be "Hollywood Night." For those occasions, the team wears a black jersey with purple letters and numbers surrounded by gold trim.

CHAPTER 3:

CATCHY NICKNAMES

QUIZ TIME!

1. By which unofficial franchise nickname have the Lakers most commonly been referred to?

   a. The Royal Stallions

   b. Smash City

   c. L.A. Legends

   d. Showtime

2. Lakers forward Elgin Baylor was known more for his offense than defense and was often referred to as "Bail-Out Baylor" for his tendency to vacate the lane when opposing forwards drove to the net.

   a. True

   b. False

3. The longtime home of the Lakers, Staples Center, has recently been referred to by media outlets as what?

   a. The Palace of Champions

   b. The House that Kobe Built

c. The Office

d. The Dock of the Bay

4. Which Lakers forward and seven-time NBA champion was nicknamed "Big Shot Bob" for his ability to hit clutch three-pointers in critical games?

a. Bobby Watson

b. Bob Boozer

c. Robert Horry

d. Robert Harrison

5. Which of the following is NOT a nickname that was bestowed upon Lakers forward Lamar Odom?

a. The Goods

b. Super Freak

c. Candy Man

d. The Package

6. Which of the following is NOT a nickname that was given to Lakers center Dwight Howard?

a. D12

b. Superman

c. The DH

d. The Daily Double

7. During his late 1970s and early 1980s heyday with the Lakers, point guard Norm Nixon was given a nickname with a political reference: "Tricky Dick," which was also applied to President Richard Nixon.

a. True

b. False

8. Why was Lakers guard Gail Goodrich given the nicknames "Stumpy" and "The Stump" by teammate Elgin Baylor?

  a. Because when he planted himself to take a charge, he was very rarely ever knocked over
  b. Because he would always give the team's pre-game "stump" speech to fire up the room
  c. Because his most common response to any question was a stumped look and a mumbled "I don't know"
  d. Because Goodrich was over 6 feet tall but had very short legs

9. Which simple rhyming nickname was given to Lakers guard Nick Van Exel thanks to his skills on the basketball court?

  a. Nick the Sick
  b. Nick the Pick
  c. Nick the Quick
  d. Nick the Slick

10. Why did Lakers center Shaquille O'Neal refer to himself in the media as "The Big Aristotle"?

  a. He wanted to be known for his intelligence as well as his obvious physicality.
  b. He loved a quote from the philosopher Aristotle, who said that "excellence is not a singular act; it's a habit. You are what you repeatedly do."
  c. He was excited about having gone back to Louisiana State University to earn his degree many years after having left early for the NBA Draft.

d. He playfully spoke about learning a great deal of philosophy under unusual coach Phil Jackson's tutelage.

11. Which Lakers player was known to fans and teammates by the nickname "Special K"?

    a. Guard Kobe Bryant
    b. Center Kareem Abdul-Jabbar
    c. Forward Kermit Washington
    d. Forward Kurt Rambis

12. After engaging in two memorable fights with his former Los Angeles teammates as a newly traded member of the New York Knicks, ex-Lakers forward Ron Artest earned the nickname "The Vengeful Ex."

    a. True
    b. False

13. Which of the following nicknames is current Lakers guard Dion Waiters NOT known to teammates by?

    a. Google Me
    b. Philly Cheese
    c. Table Ready
    d. Headache

14. Why did teammates call Lakers center Anthony Davis by the affectionate nickname "The Brow"?

    a. Because he was an academic who enjoyed high-brow cultural activities like literature groups, poetry readings, and attending the ballet

b. Because his eyebrows grew together above the peak of his nose

c. Because he was known for brow-beating his teammates on the court after they made mistakes during important games

d. Because of his trademark celebration after blocking a shot on defense; wiping the back of his hand across his brow and flicking away the sweat

15. At times during his tenure in Minneapolis, Lakers center George Mikan was referred to by all of the following nicknames except for which one?

a. Mr. Basketball

b. Big Mike

c. The Monster

d. Giant George

16. Los Angeles forward Karl Malone was called "Uncle Mailman" by his young teammates because he was brought in to provide leadership and playoff experience while demonstrating how to act as a professional athlete.

a. True

b. False

17. For what reason did teammates refer to Lakers power forward and future coach Kurt Rambis as "Clark Kent"?

a. Because he was such a go-to interview for reporters in the locker room that he was almost like a reporter himself

b. Because he wore a Superman costume to the team's 1994 Halloween party

c. Because he wore horn-rimmed black glasses that were the opposite of the flashy style of most of the Lakers

d. Because, off the court, he was never recognized around town as a Laker the way other stars were

18. Which of the following nicknames was NOT bestowed upon Hall of Fame center Wilt Chamberlain thanks to his size and skill?

    a. Wilt the Stilt
    b. The Load
    c. Giraffe Man
    d. The Record Book

19. Lakers forward Luke Walton is known by which of the following nicknames that matches his initials?

    a. Little Wheats
    b. Low Wattage
    c. Last Warrior
    d. Large Wombat

20. During his playing days, Lakers swingman Pat Riley was known as MacGyver, but when he took over as coach of the team, players called him Magnum P.I. instead.

    a. True
    b. False

QUIZ ANSWERS

1. D – Showtime

2. B – False

3. B – The House that Kobe Built

4. C – Robert Horry

5. B – Super Freak

6. C – The DH

7. B – False

8. D – Because Goodrich was over 6 feet tall but had very short legs

9. C – Nick the Quick

10. B – He loved a quote from the philosopher Aristotle, who said that "excellence is not a singular act; it's a habit. You are what you repeatedly do."

11. C – Forward Kermit Washington

12. B – False

13. C – Table Ready

14. B – Because his eyebrows grew together above the peak of his nose

15. D – Giant George

16. B – False

17. C – Because he wore horn-rimmed black glasses that were the opposite of the flashy style of most of the Lakers

18. C – Giraffe Man

19. A – Little Wheats

20. B – False

DID YOU KNOW?

1. Los Angeles forward James Worthy was no stranger to crucial games in front of large audiences. He won the NCAA Championship while taking home the NCAA Final Four Most Outstanding Player award, then won the NBA championship while winning NBA Finals MVP. All of this earned him the appropriate moniker "Big Game James."

2. Lakers coach Willem van Breda Kolff was commonly known by the short form of his name, "Bill," but nearly every Lakers fan knows him instead by his nickname "Butch."

3. Dennis "The Worm" Rodman had a short stay in Los Angeles, lasting just part of one season. Rodman earned his nickname during previous stops in his NBA career for the way he wriggled like a worm when working the flippers on pinball machines.

4. LeBron James was thought of as an all-time great basketball player while he was still in high school and, incredibly, only boosted his reputation through the years. By the time the forward arrived in Los Angeles and led the team to another championship, he was already known by the well-earned nickname "King James."

5. Lakers guard Kobe Bryant was such an iconic figure that he went by many nicknames over the years. While his favorite was "Black Mamba" (he tried to trademark the term),

Bryant was also known as "KB24," "Vino," "Showboat," "The Eighth Man," and "Little Flying Warrior."

6. Superstar guard Earvin Johnson was so well known by his nickname, "Magic," that people often forgot his given name. Johnson earned the moniker while he was still in high school, when a journalist saw him record a triple-double and making it look effortless.

7. Known for his leadership and reliability in addition to his immense talent, Kareem Abdul-Jabbar was quickly dubbed "The Captain" in Los Angeles and took pride in rarely letting the team down.

8. When point guard Gary Payton came to the Lakers, the team was stacked with plenty of scoring talent, which was okay with Payton. He came to dish out assists and play his trademark tight defense, sticking to opposing shooters so closely that he was called "The Glove."

9. The history of Shaquille O'Neal's nicknames is a long one. He has cycled through "Shaq," "Superman," "Diesel," "M.D.E" (Most Dominant Ever), "L.C.L" (Last Center Left), "Wilt Chamberneazy," "Osama Bin Shaq," "The Big Aristotle," "The Big Deporter," "The Big Felon," and "The Big Sidekick."

10. Lakers coach Phil Jackson had a history of managing egos and temperamental players. He calmed feuds like the one between center Shaquille O'Neal and guard Kobe Bryant that threatened to tear teams apart. For all of these capabilities, Jackson was dubbed "The Zen Master."

CHAPTER 4:

ALMA MATERS

QUIZ TIME!

1. Hall of Fame power forward Vern Mikkelsen was not as highly scouted as many other players, because he attended which little known school?

    a. Hamline University

    b. University of Wisconsin-River Falls

    c. Swarthmore College

    d. Arkansas Tech University

2. The Lakers have drafted more players from the Michigan State Spartans than from the Michigan Wolverines.

    a. True

    b. False

3. Forward A.C. Green played four years of college ball for which program before being drafted by the Los Angeles Lakers?

    a. Connecticut Huskies

    b. Wyoming Cowboys

c. Oregon State Beavers

d. Arizona State Sun Devils

4. First-ever Minneapolis Lakers draft choice Chuck Hanger attended the University of California, where he played for the basketball team that went by which nickname?

a. Golden Bears

b. Mountain Lions

c. Tiger Sharks

d. Thunder Cats

5. The Lakers have drafted six players from the following college basketball programs. Only one of those players, center Derrick Caracter, made it to the NBA. Which school did he come from?

a. Texas Longhorns

b. Texas A&M Aggies

c. Texas Tech Red Raiders

d. Texas-El Paso Miners

6. Which University of New Mexico Lobo was the only Lakers draftee from that school to have a successful NBA career with the team?

a. Forward Julius Randle

b. Center Elden Campbell

c. Guard Michael Cooper

d. Center Cedric Ceballos

7. Fan-favorite point guard Jerry West is the only player the Lakers have ever selected who played in college for the West Virginia Mountaineers.

a. True

b. False

8. In 1984, the Lakers drafted Richard Haenisch, who played for Chaminade University of Honolulu, in the 7ᵗʰ round. What was his college team's nickname?

   a. The Pineapples
   b. The Rainbows
   c. The Silverswords
   d. The Surfers

9. The Lakers selected two teammates from the Rice University Owls in back-to-back rounds in the 1954 NBA Draft. Which teammates did they choose with the 27ᵗʰ and 36ᵗʰ picks?

   a. Dick Garmaker and Chuck Mencel
   b. Don Lance and Gene Schwinger
   c. John Patzwald and Jim Springer
   d. Clyde Lovellette and Lew Hitch

10. Top overall pick Elgin Baylor played his college basketball as the small forward for which program before coming to the Lakers?

    a. Kansas Jayhawks
    b. Miami (Ohio) University Redhawks
    c. Southeast Missouri State Redhawks
    d. Seattle University Redhawks

11. Only two Ivy League players have played for the Lakers after being drafted by them. Which intelligent players made it with Los Angeles?

a. Jim McMillan of Columbia and Rudy LaRusso of Dartmouth

b. George Farley of Cornell and Luke Walton of Yale

c. Mark Madsen of Harvard and Eric Van Dyke of Princeton

d. Robert Sacre of Pennsylvania and Roger Brown of Brown

12. The Lakers have used the "prep-to-pro" method of drafting by selecting a player right out of high school.

   a. True

   b. False

13. Center Elden Campbell was drafted by the Lakers out of which school that is better known as a football powerhouse than a basketball school?

   a. Clemson University

   b. Louisiana State University

   c. University of Alabama

   d. University of Miami

14. The Lakers drafted two players from the Cincinnati Bearcats who went on to play more than 600 NBA games each. Who were these successful players?

   a. Center Rick Roberson and forward Elgin Baylor

   b. Guard Nick Van Exel and swingman Ruben Patterson

   c. Forward Jim Holstein and guard Derek Fisher

   d. Guard Jerry West and center Vlade Divac

15. Which player, drafted by the Lakers from the Duke University Blue Devils, went on to have the most impactful NBA career?

    a. Center Jay Buckley
    b. Guard Howard Hunt
    c. Forward Brandon Ingram
    d. Forward Ryan Kelly

16. Power forward Bill Hewitt, who was chosen 11th overall in 1968, is the highest-drafted player the Lakers have ever selected from the University of Southern California Trojans.

    a. True
    b. False

17. In which college program did Ukrainian small forward Sviatoslav Mykhailiuk play before his entrance into the NBA in 2018?

    a. New Mexico Lobos
    b. Florida State Seminoles
    c. Kentucky Wildcats
    d. Kansas Jayhawks

18. The only selection made by the Lakers from the Niagara University Purple Eagles in franchise history was used on which player?

    a. Guard Andre Turner
    b. Forward Boo Ellis
    c. Forward George Stone
    d. Forward Jack Gillespie

19. The high-scoring James Worthy was a member of which college squad before his time on the court with the Lakers?

    a. University of Memphis Tigers
    b. University of Maryland Terrapins
    c. University of North Carolina Tar Heels
    d. University of Florida Gators

20. Though the Villanova Wildcats are a perennial contender for the NCAA's March Madness tournament, the Lakers have never drafted a player from that school in their entire franchise history.

    a. True
    b. False

QUIZ ANSWERS

1. A – Hamline University

2. B – False

3. C – Oregon State Beavers

4. A – Golden Bears

5. D – Texas-El Paso Miners

6. C – Guard Michael Cooper

7. B – False

8. C – The Silverswords

9. B – Don Lance and Gene Schwinger

10. D – Seattle University Redhawks

11. A – Jim McMillan of Columbia and Rudy LaRusso of Dartmouth

12. A – True

13. A – Clemson University

14. B – Guard Nick Van Exel and swingman Ruben Patterson

15. C – Forward Brandon Ingram

16. A – True

17. D – Kansas Jayhawks

18. B – Forward Boo Ellis

19. C – University of North Carolina Tar Heels

20. B – False

DID YOU KNOW?

1. Norm Nixon, the point guard who excelled with Los Angeles before Magic Johnson arrived but was traded away afterward, remains the only player the team has ever selected from the Duquesne Dukes.

2. Los Angeles has made two Ohio State Buckeyes players top 15 picks in the NBA Draft. The team selected point guard Jim Cleamons 13th overall in 1971 and point guard D'Angelo Russel 2nd overall in 2015.

3. For a four-year stretch, from 2004 through 2007, the Lakers drafted at least one player who did not attend an American university or college. The strategy paid off, as all five of the players they selected made it to the NBA.

4. Small forward Travis Grant remains the only Kentucky State University Thorobred ever taken by the Los Angeles Lakers in an NBA Draft. The team selected Grant in the 1st round, 13th overall, in 1972.

5. Neither the Minneapolis nor the Los Angeles version of the Lakers franchise has ever selected a basketball player from the Georgetown Hoyas.

6. Gustavus Adolphus College is not a well-known school, but during the 1950s, the Lakers selected four of its players within four years. Scouting the school did not help, though, as none of them ever played in the NBA.

7. The most players Los Angeles has drafted from any school is 15. This mark is held by the University of Minnesota Golden Gophers. Eleven of those choices came in the 1950s, but the best choice was guard Archie Clark, whom the Lakers drafted in 1966.

8. In 1970, the Lakers drafted small forward Larry Mikan from the University of Minnesota. Mikan was the son of franchise legend George Mikan, who attended DePaul University. Larry played in 53 career games with the club.

9. Small forward Devean George was lucky to be noticed by NBA scouts. George played at Augsburg College, a small school that does not traditionally receive much attention from NBA teams.

10. The Lakers have drafted 11 players from the University of California-Los Angeles Bruins, and seven of these local products went on to play in the NBA. The most successful of them were all guards (Gail Goodrich, Walt Hazzard, Jordan Farmar, and Lonzo Ball).

CHAPTER 5:

STATISTICALLY SPEAKING

QUIZ TIME!

1. What is Los Angeles's franchise record for most victories by the club in a regular season?

    a. 64

    b. 66

    c. 67

    d. 69

2. No one in Lakers history is within 3,000 assists of point guard Magic Johnson at the top of the Lakers' record book.

    a. True

    b. False

3. Five players have recorded over 6,000 career rebounds for the Lakers. Who has the most?

    a. Center Wilt Chamberlain

    b. Forward Elgin Baylor

    c. Center Kareem Abdul-Jabbar

    d. Guard Magic Johnson

4. Who is the Lakers' single-season leader with 2,832 points scored?

   a. Forward Elgin Baylor
   b. Guard Jerry West
   c. Guard Kobe Bryant
   d. Center Kareem Abdul-Jabbar

5. This Laker really made his shots count, showing his accuracy with the highest career shooting percentage for the team.

   a. Center Dwight Howard
   b. Center Andrew Bynum
   c. Forward James Worthy
   d. Center JaVale McGee

6. The most personal fouls committed in a season by a Lakers player is 324. Which aggressive player established this club record?

   a. Forward Vern Mikkelsen
   b. Center Jim Chones
   c. Forward Rick Fox
   d. Center Mel Counts

7. Lakers guard Kobe Bryant attempted more than twice the number of career free throws for the Lakers as center Shaquille O'Neal, who is in second place on the franchise list.

   a. True
   b. False

8. Which player holds the Los Angeles record with 393 blocks in a single season?

    a. Center Elmore Smith
    b. Center Kareem Abdul-Jabbar
    c. Center Shaquille O'Neal
    d. Forward Elgin Baylor

9. Which Laker has played more NBA games with the franchise than anyone else?

    a. Guard Kobe Bryant
    b. Guard Jerry West
    c. Center Kareem Abdul-Jabbar
    d. Forward James Worthy

10. Kobe Bryant is Los Angeles's all-time leader in points scored with how many points?

    a. 27,840
    b. 29,613
    c. 33,643
    d. 38,922

11. Bryant also holds the single-season Lakers record for points per game. How many per-game points did he average during the 2005-06 season?

    a. 29.4
    b. 31.3
    c. 35.4
    d. 39.2

12. Bryant *missed* more field goals during his Lakers career than any other Los Angeles player has even *attempted.*

    a. True

    b. False

13. Which Lakers shooter sank the most free throws while playing with the club?

    a. Guard Magic Johnson

    b. Center Shaquille O'Neal

    c. Guard Jerry West

    d. Guard Kobe Bryant

14. On the Lakers' top 10 list for points scored by a player in a season, how many times does Kareem Abdul-Jabbar's name appear?

    a. 0

    b. 3

    c. 5

    d. 9

15. How many Lakers have had over 10,000 field goal attempts for the club during their careers?

    a. 2

    b. 4

    c. 6

    d. 8

16. Guard Kobe Bryant hit 180 three-pointers during the 2005-06 season, the franchise record.

    a. True

    b. False

17. Which Laker recorded the highest career three-point shooting percentage with the franchise, at 42.2?

   a. Forward Vladimir Radmanovic
   b. Point guard Steve Nash
   c. Forward Robert Horry
   d. Shooting guard Kobe Bryant

18. Which Laker recorded the most rebounds in one season for the team, with 1,712?

   a. Center Kareem Abdul-Jabbar
   b. Center Shaquille O'Neal
   c. Center Wilt Chamberlain
   d. Forward Dennis Rodman

19. Which two teammates posted the highest combined steals total in a season for the Lakers, with 340?

   a. Guard Eddie Jones and forward Jerome Kersey
   b. Guards Sedale Threatt and Byron Scott
   c. Guards Norm Nixon and Magic Johnson
   d. Guard Kobe Bryant and forward Robert Horry

20. Coach Bill Sharman's 1971-72 season is the benchmark for winning percentage; the team won 84.1% of their games that season.

   a. True
   b. False

QUIZ ANSWERS

1. D – 69

2. A – True

3. B – Forward Elgin Baylor

4. C – Guard Kobe Bryant

5. D – Center JaVale McGee

6. B – Center Jim Chones

7. B – False

8. A – Center Elmore Smith

9. A – Guard Kobe Bryant

10. C – 33,643

11. C – 35.4

12. B – False

13. D – Guard Kobe Bryant

14. A – 0

15. D – 8

16. B – False

17. B – Point guard Steve Nash

18. C – Center Wilt Chamberlain

19. C – Guards Norm Nixon and Magic Johnson

20. A – True

DID YOU KNOW?

1. Four players have scored more than 20,000 points with the Lakers franchise. Forward Elgin Baylor has just over 23,000, center Kareem Abdul-Jabbar just over 24,000, and guard Jerry West just over 25,000. But they all significantly trail guard Kobe Bryant, who sits at the top of the list with 33,643 points.

2. Four Los Angeles Lakers trail Chicago Bulls icon Michael Jordan on the all-time list for most points per game. Jordan is a few points ahead of Jerry West, Elgin Baylor, and LeBron James. He leads the second-place player, center Wilt Chamberlain, by just 0.05 points per game.

3. The 1966-67 season of the Lakers still stands as the roughest in team history. That year's squad committed 2,168 personal fouls to make it the most aggressive version of the club ever.

4. Giant center Kareem Abdul-Jabbar was a force in the paint for the Lakers. Abdul-Jabbar blocked 2,694 shots during his Los Angeles career to lead the franchise in that statistic. He has more than double the blocks of Shaquille O'Neal, who is in second place on that list.

5. Ultra-talented center Wilt Chamberlain often scored in bunches, which was a sight to behold. Chamberlain scored 50 points or more in 118 games. For context, superstar Bulls guard Michael Jordan is second on the list, with just 31.

6. Center Kareem Abdul-Jabbar leads the Lakers franchise in both offensive and defensive rebounds. Interestingly, Abdul-Jabbar is not the Lakers' leader in total rebounds. Forward Elgin Baylor finished his career with over 1,000 more than Kareem, but in Baylor's playing days, the NBA did not track offensive and defensive boards separately.

7. Center Wilt Chamberlain holds a comfortable lead for the top spot in the Lakers' record books when it comes to minutes per game. The indefatigable Chamberlain averaged 43.7 minutes per game during his Los Angeles career and also had four of the top five seasons in that regard, reaching a peak of 45.3 minutes a night in the 1968-69 season.

8. The Lakers twice sank more than 800 three-pointers in a season. Most recently, they did it in 2018-19 when they tallied 847, breaking the former team record of 822, set in 2017-18.

9. The deadliest Laker from the free-throw line was small forward Cazzie Russell. He shot a team record 87.7% from the stripe, just 0.1% more than guard Sasha Vujacic.

10. In 1962-63, forward Elgin Baylor had the green light and attempted 2,273 field goals, which set the franchise record for most shots taken by one player in a single season. He scored 1,029 times, which was the only time a Laker has recorded over 1,000 field goals in a season.

CHAPTER 6

THE TRADE MARKET

QUIZ TIME!

1. One of the first players acquired in a trade after the Lakers franchise moved to Los Angeles was big man Ron Johnson, whom the Lakers acquired from which team on December 17, 1960?

    a. Philadelphia Warriors
    b. St. Louis Hawks
    c. Detroit Pistons
    d. Boston Celtics

2. Los Angeles has never completed a trade with the Orlando Magic.

    a. True
    b. False

3. In 1957, the Lakers traded star center Clyde Lovellette to the Rochester Royals. Which famously nicknamed player did they receive in return?

    a. Guard "Hot Rod" Hundley
    b. Guard "Hondo" Havlicek

c. Forward "Meadowlark" Lemon

d. Guard "Pistol Pete" Maravich

4. From which team did the Lakers acquire the draft pick that they used to select legendary point guard Magic Johnson?

   a. Atlanta Hawks

   b. New Orleans Jazz

   c. Buffalo Braves

   d. Boston Celtics

5. Which useful Lakers player was NOT sent to the Philadelphia 76ers in 1968 in exchange for superstar Wilt Chamberlain?

   a. Forward Jerry Chambers

   b. Guard Archie Clark

   c. Center Darrell Imhoff

   d. Center Mel Counts

6. In one of the Lakers' best trades, they sent center Shaquille O'Neal out of L.A. in exchange for forwards Caron Butler, Brian Grant, and Lamar Odom, along with two draft picks. Which team benefitted by making this win-win deal with Los Angeles?

   a. Miami Heat

   b. Orlando Magic

   c. Boston Celtics

   d. Cleveland Cavaliers

7. Los Angeles has completed more trades with the Phoenix Suns than with any other NBA franchise.

   a. True
   b. False

8. Which Lakers coach was effectively traded to the Milwaukee Bucks for two 2nd round draft choices after the Bucks' owner offered him a massive contract to lead their team?

   a. Pat Riley
   b. Phil Jackson
   c. Mike Dunleavy Sr.
   d. Bill Sharman

9. Which of the following superstars has NOT been involved in a trade between the L.A. Lakers and Phoenix Suns?

   a. Point guard Steve Nash
   b. Swingman Pat Riley
   c. Guard Devin Booker
   d. Guard Gail Goodrich

10. Whom did the Los Angeles Lakers select with the 1982 1st round draft pick acquired from the Cleveland Cavaliers in 1980?

   a. Forward James Worthy
   b. Guard Magic Johnson
   c. Center Daniel Taylor
   d. Guard Eric Adams

11. The Lakers' famous trade for high school guard Kobe Bryant was nearly called off after which Laker refused to leave Los Angeles, decreeing that he would retire rather than play in Charlotte?

    a. Guard Eddie Jones
    b. Forward Glen Rice
    c. Center Vlade Divac
    d. Guard Nick Van Exel

12. Los Angeles has never in its history completed a trade with the Portland Trailblazers.

    a. True
    b. False

13. Which of the following players did the Lakers NOT acquire from the Orlando Magic as part of a four-team deal in which Los Angeles gave up center Andrew Bynum in 2012?

    a. Center Dwight Howard
    b. Forward Earl Clark
    c. Point guard Chris Duhon
    d. Center Josh McRoberts

14. With which other California-based NBA team have the Lakers completed the most trades?

    a. Golden State Warriors
    b. Sacramento Kings
    c. Los Angeles Clippers
    d. They have never traded with an in-state rival.

15. From which team did the Lakers acquire superstar center Kareem Abdul-Jabbar in an epic 1975 swap?

    a. Houston Rockets
    b. Milwaukee Bucks
    c. New York Knicks
    d. San Antonio Spurs

16. In 1988, the Lakers made a deal in which they received no player, draft pick, or cash. They agreed to give up a 2nd round draft choice so that the Miami Heat would not select franchise icon Kareem Abdul-Jabbar in the NBA Expansion Draft.

    a. True
    b. False

17. When the Lakers needed to trade point guard Nick Van Exel away from Los Angeles in 1998, which franchise did they send him to in order to get the two-player return that they wanted (Tyronn Lue and Tony Battie)?

    a. Cleveland Cavaliers
    b. Boston Celtics
    c. Orlando Magic
    d. Denver Nuggets

18. Which player did Los Angeles receive in return after sending former 1st overall pick Kwame Brown to the Memphis Grizzlies in 2008?

    a. Point guard Aaron McKie
    b. Forward Ruben Patterson

c. Center Pau Gasol

d. Center Chris Mihm

19. On July 6, 2019, the Lakers completed a large three-team trade, acquiring center Anthony Davis. The team sent out guards Lonzo Ball and Isaac Bonga; forwards Josh Hart, De'Andre Hunter, Brandon Ingram, and Jemerrio Jones; center Moritz Wagner; cash; three 1st round draft choices; and one 2nd round draft choice. Who were the other two teams involved in the complicated deal?

    a. Charlotte Hornets and Indiana Pacers

    b. New Orleans Pelicans and Denver Nuggets

    c. San Antonio Spurs and Golden State Warriors

    d. New Orleans Pelicans and Washington Wizards

20. The Lakers once completed a trade with the Memphis Grizzlies in which brothers Marc and Pau Gasol were exchanged for one another.

    a. True

    b. False

QUIZ ANSWERS

1. C – Detroit Pistons

2. B – False

3. A – Guard "Hot Rod" Hundley

4. B – New Orleans Jazz

5. D – Center Mel Counts

6. A – Miami Heat

7. A – True

8. C – Mike Dunleavy Sr.

9. C – Guard Devin Booker

10. A – Forward James Worthy

11. C – Center Vlade Divac

12. B – False

13. D – Center Josh McRoberts

14. C – Los Angeles Clippers

15. B – Milwaukee Bucks

16. A – True

17. D – Denver Nuggets

18. C – Center Pau Gasol

19. D – New Orleans Pelicans and Washington Wizards

20. A – True

DID YOU KNOW?

1. Los Angeles has never made a trade with its former city, Minneapolis. After the Lakers left the state of Minnesota in 1960, there was no NBA team there until the league granted Minnesota an expansion franchise in 1989. In over 30 years since then, the Lakers and Timberwolves have not made any deals.

2. The Lakers and Boston Celtics have had a fairly heated rivalry throughout their existence, particularly during the 1980s. The two teams have set aside their dislike for each other to make a trade only three times in Los Angeles's long tenure in the NBA; one each in 1977, 1999, and 2004.

3. In an interesting twist of fate, the Lakers once traded two Odoms in the same deal. On December 11, 2011, the team acquired a 1st round pick from the Dallas Mavericks for forward Lamar Odom and a 2nd round pick. That 2nd round pick was later used on guard Darius Johnson-Odom. Johnson-Odom's middle name was Earvin, as his mother had named him after Lakers great Magic Johnson. In 2012, the Lakers acquired Johnson-Odom to play for them.

4. The Lakers and New York Knicks have a long history of trades throughout the years. Significant names moved between the two teams include Slater Martin, Dick Garmaker, Bob Boozer, Doug Christie, and Glen Rice.

5. In a challenging situation, Lakers superstar Kobe Bryant

was once caught on video stating that his teammate, center Andrew Bynum, should have been traded away because Bryant preferred to play with point guard Jason Kidd instead.

6. The Lakers had made five trades with the Buffalo Braves/San Diego Clippers franchise through 1983. After the Clippers moved to Los Angeles in 1984, the two teams did not trade with each other again for 35 years before finally agreeing on a deal that brought center Mike Muscala to the Lakers in 2019.

7. One of the worst trades made by the Lakers occurred on March 10, 1999, when they sent guard Eddie Jones and center Elden Campbell to the Charlotte Hornets for guard B.J. Armstrong and forwards Glen Rice and J.R. Reid. Rice, the centerpiece of the deal for L.A., did not fit in with Lakers duo Kobe Bryant and Shaquille O'Neal and had to be shipped out of town for the good of the locker room.

8. The Lakers definitely maximized their return on center Erwin Mueller. They traded for him in January 1968 from the Chicago Bulls. A few months later, in September 1968, they shipped him back to the Bulls for a better return. L.A. gained over 11 win shares worth of surplus value through the two trades.

9. In a deal that was very unpopular at the time, Los Angeles dealt excellent center Vlade Divac, who had played with the Lakers for the first seven years of his career, to the Charlotte Hornets for a high school kid. That kid turned

out to be superstar guard Kobe Bryant, and fans forgave the team for dealing Divac.

10. One of the larger and more impactful trades ever made by the Lakers was a four-team swap completed September 20, 2000, with the New York Knicks, Seattle Supersonics, and Phoenix Suns. In all, 17 assets changed hands, including star players Patrick Ewing, Glen Rice, Horace Grant, Chuck Person, and Vernon Maxwell.

CHAPTER 7:

DRAFT DAY

QUIZ TIME!

1. Which prospect did the Lakers select 9th overall with their very first draft choice in 1948?

    a. Cliff Crandall from Oregon State
    b. Vern Mikkelsen from Hamline
    c. Chuck Hanger from California
    d. Kevin O'Shea from Notre Dame

2. The Lakers have never held the 1st overall pick in the NBA Draft in the entire history of the franchise.

    a. True
    b. False

3. How high did Los Angeles select power forward Larry Nance Jr. in the 2015 NBA Entry Draft?

    a. 1st round, 5th overall
    b. 1st round, 27th overall
    c. 2nd round, 43rd overall
    d. 7th round, 222nd overall

4. Which point guard did the Lakers select highest in the NBA Entry Draft, using a 1st overall draft choice to add the floor general to their team?

a. Magic Johnson

b. Lonzo Ball

c. Jerry West

d. Norm Nixon

5. Who was the first player ever selected by the Lakers in the NBA Entry Draft to be their lone selection for a single year?

a. Guard Gail Goodrich in 1965

b. Guard Earl Tatum in 1976

c. Guard David Rivers in 1988

d. Forward Joe Crawford in 2008

6. Which player who was drafted by the Lakers played the most NBA games?

a. Forward A.C. Green

b. Center Vlade Divac

c. Guard Derek Fisher

d. Center Elden Campbell

7. At one point, years before the 1992 NBA Draft, the Los Angeles Lakers owned the 1st overall pick that would become superstar Shaquille O'Neal. Later in O'Neal's career, he would play for the Lakers and win multiple championships.

a. True

b. False

8. The Lakers have looked to Europe for talent frequently in the NBA Entry Draft and have selected several players from the continent. Which European did they draft most recently?

    a. Center Marc Gasol from Spain
    b. Center Ivica Zubac from Croatia
    c. Guard Sasha Vujacic from Slovenia
    d. Center Vlade Divac from Serbia

9. Fan-favorite Mark Madsen was selected in the 1st round by the Los Angeles Lakers in 2000. What position did he play?

    a. Point guard
    b. Shooting guard
    c. Small forward
    d. Center

10. Who was the first player ever drafted by the Lakers who did not play for an American college team?

    a. Center Vlade Divac
    b. Guard Jay Triano
    c. Center Andrew Bynum
    d. Guard Sasha Vujacic

11. When the NBA merged with the ABA in 1976 and two teams (the Kentucky Colonels and the Spirits of St. Louis) were disbanded, whom did the Lakers select in the resulting dispersal draft?

    a. Center Artis Gilmore from Kentucky
    b. Forward Maurice Lucas from Kentucky

c. Guard Mike Barr from St. Louis

d. The Lakers passed and did not select any players.

12. Three times during the 2000s, Los Angeles has traded away all of its draft picks and chosen players on draft day.

   a. True

   b. False

13. The Lakers struck out mightily in the 1983 NBA Draft, selecting five players who scored a total of how many points in the NBA?

   a. 0

   b. 118

   c. 240

   d. 285

14. Of the draft spots in the top 10 in the NBA Draft, which spot has Los Angeles selected at more than any other?

   a. 1st overall pick

   b. 2nd overall pick

   c. 5th overall pick

   d. 10th overall pick

15. Superstar guard Jerry West was drafted by Los Angeles in the 1st round, 2nd overall, in the 1960 NBA Entry Draft. Which Hall of Fame player was selected ahead of him?

   a. Oscar Robertson of the Cincinnati Royals

   b. Nate Thurmond of the San Francisco Warriors

   c. Jerry Lucas of the Cincinnati Royals

   d. John Havlicek of the Boston Celtics

16. Magic Johnson was such a talented athlete coming out of college that he was drafted in not one but three sports (basketball, baseball, and football).

    a. True
    b. False

17. Up to and including the 2019 NBA Entry Draft, how many player selections have the Lakers made in their history?

    a. 260
    b. 305
    c. 439
    d. 581

18. How many times in history has Los Angeles used a top 10 overall draft pick?

    a. 8
    b. 15
    c. 21
    d. 29

19. What is the lowest position in the draft that Los Angeles has selected a player who would go on to make the Naismith Memorial Basketball Hall of Fame?

    a. 1st round, 2nd overall
    b. 1st round, 26th overall
    c. 2nd round, 43rd overall
    d. 7th round, 165th overall

20. There have been 26 players in the NBA who measured 7'3" or taller. The Lakers have never drafted any of them.

    a. True

    b. False

QUIZ ANSWERS

1. C – Chuck Hanger from California

2. B – False

3. B – 1st round, 27th overall

4. A – Magic Johnson

5. C – Guard David Rivers in 1988

6. C – Guard Derek Fisher

7. B – False

8. B – Center Ivica Zubac from Croatia

9. D – Center

10. B – Guard Jay Triano

11. D – The Lakers passed and did not select any players.

12. B – False

13. A – 0

14. B – 2nd overall pick

15. A – Oscar Robertson of the Cincinnati Royals

16. B – False

17. C – 439

18. D – 29

19. B – 1st round, 26th overall

20. A – True

DID YOU KNOW?

1. From 1970 to 1973, Los Angeles enjoyed an unusual stretch in which they selected at least one player per year named "Jim" who lasted 500 games in the NBA. During those years, they hit on: forward Jim McMillian, guards Jim Cleamons and Jim Price, and center Jim Chones.

2. Despite the major draft success of franchise icon Jerry West, the Lakers have only selected five other players from West Virginia. None of those players has lasted for even a full season's worth of games with Los Angeles.

3. Of all the players drafted by the Lakers, forward Elgin Baylor leads in minutes per game (40), points per game (27.4), and rebounds per game (13.5).

4. Los Angeles has drafted precisely three players who have played just one game in the NBA; Roger Strickland, George Brown, and Carl McNulty. McNulty saw the most playing time of the three, logging 14 minutes and scoring 2 points before his NBA career ended.

5. The first Lakers draft pick who went on to play 1,000 NBA games was center Leroy Ellis. Los Angeles chose him with the 6th overall selection in 1962 out of St. John's, and the decision paid off handsomely.

6. The Lakers have held the 27th overall pick 10 times, more than any other spot in the draft. They have only elected to

trade the selection once. When they kept it, their best draft pick was center Elden Campbell from Clemson. Only two of these choices have failed to play in an NBA game.

7. The largest Lakers draft class ever was in 1953, when the team drafted 18 players. The draft was not a success, however, as only two players suited up for Minneapolis. Power forward Jim Fritsche played just two games with the Lakers, and guard Ron Feiereisel lasted only 10.

8. Conversely, some of the smallest draft classes ever have been a resounding success for the Lakers. Stars like center Vlade Divac, swingman Eddie Jones, and guard Derek Fisher all went on to long and productive careers after being the only player taken by Los Angeles in their draft years.

9. In 1947, the NBA, which was called the NBL at the time, held a Professional Basketball League of America dispersal draft. The first pick was owned by the Lakers, and they used it wisely. Minneapolis selected center George Mikan, who became the player considered the "first superstar" in league history.

10. The latest pick the Lakers have made in the NBA Draft was Bob Thate from Occidental College, whom the team chose 232nd overall in 1970. Thate never made it to the NBA. The year before, Mack Calvin, the team's 187th overall pick from USC, did go on to play over 200 NBA games after a stint in the ABA. Calvin was the latest pick they've made who actually played for the team.

CHAPTER 8:

THE GUARDS

QUIZ TIME!

1. Who was the regular starting point guard for Los Angeles during the team's challenging first season after relocating from Minneapolis in 1960?

    a. Slick Leonard

    b. Jerry West

    c. Hot Rod Hundley

    d. Jim King

2. Throughout the different phases of his life, Magic Johnson held the roles of player, coach, president of basketball operations, and part-owner of the Los Angeles Lakers.

    a. True

    b. False

3. Which point guard has recorded the most career turnovers at the position while with the Los Angeles Lakers?

    a. Norm Nixon

    b. Derek Fisher

   c. Byron Scott

   d. Magic Johnson

4. Which guard has played the most minutes for the Lakers?

   a. Byron Scott

   b. Magic Johnson

   c. Kobe Bryant

   d. Jerry West

5. One of the best Lakers statistical lines in history was accomplished when a guard recorded an unofficial quadruple-double, scoring 44 points (on incredibly efficient 16 for 17 field goal attempts, along with 12 for 12 from the free-throw line), 12 rebounds, 12 assists, and 10 blocks. Who posted this fantastic box score?

   a. Magic Johnson

   b. Kobe Bryant

   c. Jerry West

   d. Norm Nixon

6. Shooting guard Kobe Bryant played his entire NBA career with the Los Angeles Lakers after they made a draft-day trade with the Charlotte Hornets to acquire him. How long did that career last?

   a. 10 seasons

   b. 15 seasons

   c. 20 seasons

   d. 25 seasons

7. It is a Lakers tradition for every point guard to lob an alley-oop for each teammate during the warm-up before a home playoff game.

   a. True
   b. False

8. Which of the following is NOT a fact about talented Lakers shooting guard Byron Scott?

   a. He went on to become the head coach of four NBA teams, including the Los Angeles Lakers.
   b. He has raised over $15 million for children's charities through the Byron Scott Children's Fund.
   c. He was raised in Inglewood, California, very close to The Forum, which was the Lakers' home at the time.
   d. He was honored by having the gymnasium named after him at his alma mater, Arizona State University.

9. Which Lakers point guard holds the franchise record for most assists recorded in a single game, with 24 passes converted into points?

   a. Magic Johnson
   b. Rajon Rondo
   c. Jerry West
   d. Derek Fisher

10. Though the origin of the term "triple-double" is disputed, many claim that it was invented by the L.A. Lakers director of public relations to describe the versatile play of which Lakers guard?

a. Jerry West

b. Robert Horry

c. Nick Van Exel

d. Magic Johnson

11. Lakers mainstay Derek Fisher played over 900 NBA games with the club. Where does he rank in games played all-time for Los Angeles?

a. 1st overall

b. 2nd overall

c. 5th overall

d. 11th overall

12. Kobe Bryant once declared to the press that he loved shooting and would not stop even if the shots were not falling, saying, "I would rather go 0 for 30 than 0 for 9."

a. True

b. False

13. Which of the following positions has popular Lakers point guard Jerry West NOT held with Los Angeles after retiring from his playing career?

a. Head coach

b. Scout

c. General manager

d. Color commentator

14. Which two of these current Lakers guards have been with the team for three seasons; the longest current tenure in Los Angeles's backcourt?

a. LeBron James and J.R. Smith

b. Kentavious Caldwell-Pope and Alex Caruso

c. Danny Green and Avery Bradley

d. Rajon Rondo and Dion Waiters

15. Which of the following facts about Lakers shooting guard Eddie Jones is NOT true?

   a. He appeared in a Taco Bell commercial which featured teammate Shaquille O'Neal dealing with "Taco Neck Syndrome."

   b. He appeared on the cover of the video game NBA Shootout '97.

   c. He appeared as a firefighter in a music video by the rap group Wu-Tang Clan.

   d. He appeared in an episode of *Pros vs. Joes* where he competed against ordinary athletes.

16. Former Lakers point guard Sedale Threatt was the first guard in NBA history to hit a three-pointer after the three-point line was approved in 1979 after years of debate.

   a. True

   b. False

17. Which Lakers guard was also a member of a rap group called Cheizaw, which was signed to a deal by Sony Entertainment, before recording his own solo album titled *Visions*?

   a. Kobe Bryant

   b. Nick Van Exel

   c. Derek Fisher

   d. Lonzo Ball

18. Los Angeles point guard Magic Johnson played for the original United States "Dream Team" in the Summer Olympics in which year?

    a. 1984
    b. 1988
    c. 1992
    d. 1996

19. Which rival guard was Kobe Bryant suspended one game for punching in 2002?

    a. Gary Payton of the Seattle Supersonics
    b. Latrell Sprewell of the Golden State Warriors
    c. Dwayne Wade of the Miami Heat
    d. Reggie Miller of the Indiana Pacers

20. Lakers guard Nick Van Exel set an interesting record by recording 39 consecutive assists to the same player (teammate Shaquille O'Neal).

    a. True
    b. False

QUIZ ANSWERS

1. B – Jerry West

2. A – True

3. D – Magic Johnson

4. C – Kobe Bryant

5. C – Jerry West

6. C – 20 seasons

7. B – False

8. D – He was honored by having the gymnasium named after him at his alma mater, Arizona State University.

9. A – Magic Johnson

10. D – Magic Johnson

11. C – 5th overall

12. A – True

13. D – Color commentator

14. B – Kentavious Caldwell-Pope and Alex Caruso

15. C – He appeared as a firefighter in a music video by the rap group Wu-Tang Clan.

16. B – False

17. A – Kobe Bryant

18. C – 1992

19. D – Reggie Miller of the Indiana Pacers

20. B – False

DID YOU KNOW?

1. From age six to 13, future Lakers superstar Kobe Bryant lived in Italy, where he began learning to play basketball and picked up the Italian language well enough to speak it fluently as an adult.

2. After superstar Lakers guard Magic Johnson was diagnosed as HIV-positive, he decided to step away from basketball to re-evaluate his situation. Though Johnson later returned, during the interim period, the Lakers turned to Sedale Threatt to step in at point guard.

3. Hall of Fame Lakers guard Charlie Scott had a good head for business too. After his playing career, Scott became a marketing director for the very popular athletic wear company Champion.

4. Kobe Bryant, star guard for the Los Angeles Lakers, appeared on the cover of nine different video games, all of which were NBA-related.

5. During his retirement from the NBA, Lakers guard Magic Johnson formed the Magic Johnson All-Stars, a team of other former NBA players who toured America, Israel, Australia, Europe, South America, Japan, and New Zealand.

6. Lakers legend Jerry West was an iconic figure during his playing years in Los Angeles. West was so iconic that the

NBA logo is based on a silhouette of him driving to the basket.

7. Seven point guards who have played for the Lakers have been enshrined in the Basketball Hall of Fame. The most recent was Canadian star Steve Nash, who was elected in 2018.

8. Lakers guard Jerry West was presented with the Presidential Medal of Freedom by American President Donald Trump in the Oval Office at the White House in 2019.

9. Magic Johnson was an incredible winner on the basketball court. He won a high school championship and an NCAA Championship with Michigan State, before winning an NBA title with the Lakers in his rookie year. Johnson was even named Finals MVP that year, before earning four more championships with the team.

10. The Lakers record for most points in a single game was set by guard Kobe Bryant on January 22, 2006, when the team faced off against the Toronto Raptors. Bryant poured in 81 points (66% of his team's total output) in a 122-104 victory. This was the second-highest scoring game in NBA history, behind only Wilt Chamberlain's 100-point outburst over 40 years previously.

CHAPTER 9:

CENTERS OF ATTENTION

QUIZ TIME!

1. Where was former Lakers center Kareem Abdul-Jabbar born?

   a. Kinshasa, Democratic Republic of Congo
   b. Paris, France
   c. New York City
   d. Los Angeles

2. L.A. Lakers center Elden Campbell, who played nine years with the team, was born and raised in Los Angeles.

   a. True
   b. False

3. Vlade Divac, who was one of the first Europeans in the NBA during his time with the Lakers, freely admitted to using which questionable tactic to gain an edge during games?

   a. Sticking his foot underneath the legs of a jumping shooter to create a potential injury when the shooter landed

b. Flopping when an opponent bumped into him, trying to draw a foul call

c. Deliberately wiping his sweat on opponents so that they would be less likely to guard him closely

d. Discreetly grabbing the shorts of opponents when they posted him up so that they would be unable to jump near the rim

4. Center Shaquille O'Neal was a key member of three championship teams in Los Angeles, but also won a fourth NBA title with which other franchise?

   a. Orlando Magic
   b. Cleveland Cavaliers
   c. Boston Celtics
   d. Miami Heat

5. Which Lakers coach/center duo once had a motivational exchange in which the coach told the player "the MVP trophy should be named after (you) when (you) retire"?

   a. Pat Riley and Kareem Abdul-Jabbar
   b. Phil Jackson and Shaquille O'Neal
   c. Bill Sharman and Wilt Chamberlain
   d. Pat Riley and Vlade Divac

6. Which well-known Lakers center also spent time playing basketball for the Harlem Globetrotters?

   a. Wilt Chamberlain
   b. Kareem Abdul-Jabbar
   c. Shaquille O'Neal
   d. Vlade Divac

7. For 10 years, the NCAA banned slam dunks from being used in college games, because Kareem Abdul-Jabbar was so difficult to stop when dunking.

    a. True
    b. False

8. Before he became a Muslim and changed his name to reflect his new faith, what was Kareem Abdul-Jabbar's name?

    a. Lou David Williams
    b. Kenneth Aaron Johnson
    c. Wilbur Donovan
    d. Ferdinand Lewis Alcindor Jr.

9. What was the term given to the strategy that opposing teams used to slow down Lakers center Shaquille O'Neal, who was a notoriously bad free-throw shooter?

    a. The O'Neal Oh No
    b. The Shaq Psyche
    c. The Hack-a-Shaq
    d. The Brick Layer

10. Which of the following is NOT a fact about Lakers center Kareem Abdul-Jabbar?

    a. He played a key role as pilot Roger Murdock in a satirical 1980 movie called *Airplane!*.
    b. He trained in martial arts with the legendary Bruce Lee.
    c. He was appointed a U.S. global cultural ambassador by Secretary of State Hillary Clinton.

d. He could slam dunk basketballs by the time he was in the fifth grade

11. Iconic Lakers center Shaquille O'Neal also released six rap albums in his spare time. Which of these albums became a platinum-selling hit record?

a. Shaq Fu: Da Return
b. Shaq Diesel
c. Shoot Pass Slam!
d. You Can't Stop the Reign

12. Los Angeles pivot Wilt Chamberlain led the NBA in field goal percentage in three different seasons with the Lakers.

a. True
b. False

13. What was the nickname used around the league for Lakers center Kareem Abdul-Jabbar's most common and effective shot?

a. The Perfect J
b. The Glass and Rim
c. The Skyhook
d. The Fadeaway

14. After his basketball career ended, which sport did Lakers pivot Wilt Chamberlain play well enough to make that sport's hall of fame?

a. Pole vaulting
b. Table tennis
c. Curling
d. Volleyball

15. Which of the following statements about Lakers center Benoit Benjamin is NOT true?

   a. Commentator Dick Vitale once claimed that Benjamin wore 00 because it symbolized his intensity level.

   b. Benjamin once showed up for a game with two left shoes.

   c. Benjamin provoked a fight in practice with teammate Eddie Jones by exclaiming "Benoit!" every time he sank a shot over Jones.

   d. Benjamin used famous boxing promoter Don King as one of his agents.

16. No Lakers center has ever led the team in points scored during a single game.

   a. True

   b. False

17. During center Kareem Abdul-Jabbar's final NBA game against the Boston Celtics, the teams agreed to play by which two unusual, unofficial rules?

   a. Each Laker had to get at least one assist passing to Abdul-Jabbar and each Celtic had to commit at least one foul on him to put him on the free-throw line.

   b. No Celtic was allowed to block any of Abdul-Jabbar's shots outside the paint, and in return, no Laker would attempt to rebound the ball if he missed.

   c. Each player wore Abdul-Jabbar's number, 33, in tribute and each temporarily switched to an Islamic name for the night.

d. Each player had to wear goggles and attempt at least one skyhook.

18. Kareem Abdul-Jabbar was considered the greatest basketball player in history by which of his contemporaries?

    a. Coach Phil Jackson, Boston Celtic Larry Bird, and New York Knick Patrick Ewing
    b. Coach Pat Riley, Philadelphia 76er Julius Erving, and Detroit Piston Isiah Thomas
    c. Coach Jerry Sloan, Utah Jazz Karl Malone, and San Antonio Spur David Robinson
    d. Coach John Wooden, Los Angeles Laker Magic Johnson, and Houston Rocket Hakeem Olajuwon

19. Which Lakers center played one incredibly dominant season, becoming one of only three players to win the NBA Most Valuable Player, NBA Finals Most Valuable Player, and NBA All-Star Game Most Valuable Player in the same season?

    a. Andrew Bynum
    b. Kareem Abdul-Jabbar
    c. Shaquille O'Neal
    d. Wilt Chamberlain

20. Lakers big man Shaquille O'Neal was also actively involved in law enforcement. Over the course of a decade, O'Neal became a reserve officer for the L.A. Port Police, a U.S. deputy marshal, and a sheriff's deputy.

    a. True
    b. False

QUIZ ANSWERS

1. C – New York City

2. A – True

3. B – Flopping when an opponent bumped into him, trying to draw a foul call

4. D – Miami Heat

5. B – Phil Jackson and Shaquille O'Neal

6. A – Wilt Chamberlain

7. A – True

8. D – Ferdinand Lewis Alcindor Jr.

9. C – The Hack-a-Shaq

10. D – He could slam dunk basketballs by the time he was in the fifth grade.

11. B – Shaq Diesel

12. A – True

13. C – The Skyhook

14. D – Volleyball

15. C – Benjamin provoked a fight in practice with teammate Eddie Jones by exclaiming "Benoit!" every time he sank a shot over Jones.

16. B – False

17. D – Each player had to wear goggles and attempt at least one skyhook.

18. B – Coach Pat Riley, Philadelphia 76er Julius Erving, and Detroit Piston Isiah Thomas

19. C – Shaquille O'Neal

20. A – True

DID YOU KNOW?

1. In a 20-year career, the only NBA All-Star Game in which Lakers center Kareem Abdul-Jabbar did not participate was in 1978. Even then, Abdul-Jabbar's skills were good enough for him to be in the game, but he had a broken hand and could not play.

2. The only NBA player ever to average at least 30 points and 20 rebounds in any season is Lakers center Wilt Chamberlain. Chamberlain was so consistently excellent that he is also the only player to average these numbers for a full career.

3. Lakers center Andrew Bynum holds the record as the youngest person to play in an NBA game. Bynum was drafted out of high school and played for Los Angeles at 18 years and 6 days old. The record had previously been held by Lakers guard Kobe Bryant.

4. During his rookie season in the NBA, future Lakers center Shaquille O'Neal twice dunked the ball so powerfully that it destroyed the backboard, causing the NBA to strengthen the backboard after the season.

5. Center Wilt Chamberlain, at a very athletic 7'1" tall, was capable of dunking from the free-throw line without any run-up approach. Both the NBA and the NCAA banned this technique for free throws as a result of Chamberlain's dominance.

6. Before playing for the Lakers, Kareem Abdul-Jabbar won three NCAA championships as a UCLA Bruins starter. He is one of just four college players who started for three title winners during their college careers.

7. Serbian Lakers pivot Vlade Divac was the first player born and raised in a country other than America to play over 1,000 NBA games. He is also one of just four Europeans whose number has been retired by an NBA team (though, for Divac, it was the Sacramento Kings, not the Lakers).

8. After Kareem Abdul-Jabbar's house burned down in a fire, he mentioned that he was most upset about losing his collection of over 3,000 jazz records. Lakers fans responded by sending him replacement albums in a show of gratitude and respect for his place with the franchise.

9. A larger-than-life personality, Wilt Chamberlain often boasted (including in his autobiography) about having sex with 20,000 women.

10. During Kareem Abdul-Jabbar's first season with the Lakers after his acquisition from the Milwaukee Bucks, Abdul-Jabbar left a lasting impression on his new hometown and the league. He hauled in 1,111 defensive rebounds; a record which still stands 45 years later.

CHAPTER 10:

THE FORWARDS

QUIZ TIME!

1. Small forward LeBron James switched to which other position with the Lakers in 2020, changing his game effectively around his teammates to lead them to an NBA championship and win NBA Finals Most Valuable Player?

    a. Center
    b. Power forward
    c. Shooting guard
    d. Point guard

2. The Lakers have had more forwards elected to the Basketball Hall of Fame than any other position.

    a. True
    b. False

3. Why did forward Elgin Baylor play just 48 games during the 1961-62 NBA season?

    a. The season was shortened due to a players' strike which was not resolved in time to complete a full schedule.

b. Baylor injured his right knee during a Lakers practice at the beginning of the year and could not return for months.

c. Baylor was summoned for active duty in the U.S. military and could only play on weekends when he was granted leave.

d. Baylor sat out specific games against teams that had not integrated in order to protest racial inequality.

4. What was forward Jim Pollard's claim to fame during his amateur baseball career in Minnesota, which took place during his offseason from the Lakers?

   a. He struck out Joe DiMaggio when DiMaggio was on a rehab assignment.

   b. He "hit a ball that didn't stop until it got to Chicago" after it landed in one of the cars of a passing train.

   c. He stole 100 bases in a single season (second base 50 times and third base 50 times).

   d. He was the catcher during a no-hitter pitched by Baseball Hall-of-Famer Satchel Paige.

5. The initials in popular Lakers forward A.C. Green's name stand for what?

   a. Arthur Charles

   b. Anthony Christopher

   c. Amanda Chester

   d. Ahmed Cruz

6. Which Lakers forward has had his number retired by the Lakers, his college basketball team, and two different high schools?

   a. Elgin Baylor
   b. Jamaal Wilkes
   c. Karl Malone
   d. Robert Horry

7. Lakers forward Tom Hawkins went on to a post-playing career with the Los Angeles Dodgers, for whom he was vice president of communications.

   a. True
   b. False

8. Lakers forward LeBron James was the first player in NBA history to accomplish which of the following feats?

   a. Win an NBA championship with three different franchises
   b. Be named All-Star Game's Most Valuable Player for both conferences
   c. Play all five positions during an NBA playoff game
   d. Record a triple-double against every franchise in the NBA

9. About which forward did Minneapolis Lakers owner Bob Short say, after signing the player to a large contract to boost attendance and save the franchise: "If he had turned me down then, I would have been out of business. The club would have gone bankrupt."?

a. Vern Mikkelsen
b. Jim Pollard
c. Elgin Baylor
d. Jerry Chambers

10. What caused the Phoenix Suns to trade forward Robert Horry to the Los Angeles Lakers in 1997, giving the Lakers a clutch shooter who helped them win three NBA championships?

   a. The Suns acquired forward Charles Barkley, an MVP candidate whose presence made Horry expendable.
   b. Horry demanded a contract extension worth more than the Suns were able to fit into their salary cap.
   c. Phoenix fans booed Horry after some disparaging remarks he made about teammate Sam Cassell in a post-game interview.
   d. Horry flung a towel at Suns coach Danny Ainge during an argument on the court.

11. Which of the following is NOT a fact about Elgin Baylor's 22 seasons as vice president of basketball operations for the Los Angeles Clippers?

   a. He filed a lawsuit alleging discrimination against team owner Donald Sterling based on the lack of adequate compensation due to his race and age.
   b. He traded regularly with the Los Angeles Lakers, making 15 deals during this time that involved 56 players and nine draft picks.
   c. His teams had a win-loss record of 607-1,153, and

only posted two regular seasons with a winning record.

    d. The Clippers won just a single playoff series during Baylor's tenure at the helm.

12. Lakers forward Rick Fox has a second career as a professional actor. Fox has appeared in over 50 motion pictures and television shows since 1994.

    a. True

    b. False

13. Which of the following is NOT a fact about forward Lamar Odom?

    a. Odom was married to television personality Khloe Kardashian and appeared frequently on her reality series, *Keeping Up with the Kardashians,* before the two started their own reality series.

    b. Odom was once described by Lakers general manager Mitch Kupchak as "the most popular player in our locker room."

    c. Odom was once found unconscious in a brothel in Nevada and spent time in a coma recovering in a hospital afterward.

    d. Odom is a noted adrenaline junkie who has participated in bungee jumping, skydiving, speedboat racing, MMA fighting, and swimming with sharks.

14. In 2008, LeBron James became the first black man to appear on the cover of which publication?

    a. *Vogue* magazine

    b. Cigar Aficionado magazine

c. *Playboy* magazine

d. The Hockey News magazine

15. Which Hall of Fame Lakers forward went on to win the NBA's Executive of the Year award with the Los Angeles Clippers?

   a. Lamar Odom

   b. Jim Pollard

   c. Elgin Baylor

   d. Vern Mikkelsen

16. Lakers forward Robert Horry won three NBA championships with the club, two with the Houston Rockets, and two more with the San Antonio Spurs. Horry's seven rings is more than any other NBA player who was not a part of the 1960s Boston Celtics dynasty.

   a. True

   b. False

17. Which type of slam dunk was decorated Lakers forward James Worthy best known for completing on fast breaks?

   a. The sidearm windmill dunk

   b. The Statue of Liberty dunk

   c. The two-handed reverse dunk

   d. The alley-oop dunk

18. Longtime Lakers forward Rick Fox holds dual nationality from which two countries?

   a. America and France

   b. Israel and America

c. Great Britain and Sweden

d. Canada and Bahamas

19. Which of the following is NOT a fact about Lakers forward A.C. Green, a devout Christian who was legendarily well behaved?

    a. Throughout all levels of his education, Green has perfect attendance with zero classes missed.

    b. Green is a member of the World Sports Humanitarian Hall of Fame.

    c. One hour before and one hour after every single Lakers road game, Green called home to speak with his mother.

    d. Despite the opportunities that came with being a famous Laker, Green remained a virgin from the time he entered the league until the time he left the league 16 years later.

20. The Lakers drafted star forward Elgin Baylor more than once. The team selected him in 1956 in the 14th round of the NBA Draft, and then later selected him 1st overall in 1958.

    a. True

    b. False

QUIZ ANSWERS

1. D – Point guard

2. A – True

3. C – Baylor was summoned for active duty in the U.S. military and could only play on weekends when he was granted leave.

4. B – He "hit a ball that didn't stop until it got to Chicago" after it landed in one of the cars of a passing train.

5. C – Amanda Chester

6. B – Jamaal Wilkes

7. A – True

8. D – Record a triple-double against every franchise in the NBA

9. C – Elgin Baylor

10. D – Horry flung a towel at Suns coach Danny Ainge during an argument on the court.

11. B – He traded regularly with the Los Angeles Lakers, making 15 deals during this time that involved 56 players and nine draft picks.

12. A – True

13. D – Odom is a noted adrenaline junkie who has participated in bungee jumping, skydiving, speedboat racing, MMA fighting, and swimming with sharks.

14. A – *Vogue* magazine

15. C – Elgin Baylor

16. A – True

17. B – The Statue of Liberty dunk

18. D – Canada and Bahamas

19. C – One hour before and one hour after every single Lakers road game, Green called home to speak with his mother.

20. A – True

DID YOU KNOW?

1. A.C. Green was diagnosed with chronic hiccups. During his time in Los Angeles, they would subside only if he was playing, exercising, or running. The condition prevented Green from sleeping longer than a couple of hours continuously.

2. Lakers forward Rudy LaRusso was very well-rounded. In addition to his basketball skills, he was also an Ivy League graduate and once made an appearance on the hit television show *Gilligan's Island*.

3. Minneapolis forward Vern Mikkelsen was relentless on defense, to the point where it often cost him. For three consecutive seasons, he led the NBA in the number of games in which he fouled out, and his career record of fouling out 127 times still stands.

4. Lakers forward Jamaal Wilkes earned some of the highest praise possible from perhaps the best collegiate coach in history, UCLA's John Wooden. Wooden was asked about the qualities he wanted in the perfect player, and said: "I would have the player be a good student, polite, courteous, a good team player, a good defensive player and rebounder, a good inside player and outside shooter...why not just take Jamaal Wilkes and let it go at that?".

5. "Big Game James" Worthy was always counted on during the Showtime era of Lakers basketball. He could be

counted on to step up his game in the playoffs, leading the star-studded team in scoring during two of those title years and averaging a full 3.5 more points per game in the playoffs than in the regular season.

6. In 2019, Lakers forward LeBron James filed a request for a trademark of the term "Taco Tuesday" after displaying pictures of his family's Mexican cuisine on the social media platform Instagram. The United States Patent and Trademark Office denied James's application on the grounds that the term was too commonly used.

7. Much like center Kareem Abdul-Jabbar, Lakers forward Jamaal Wilkes converted to Islam during his playing career. Although he still wore "Wilkes" on the back of his jersey, he legally changed his name to Jamaal Abdul-Lateef in 1975.

8. James Worthy was incredibly talented, but he was also lucky to be blessed with great teammates. Not only did Worthy play with point guard Magic Johnson and center Kareem Abdul-Jabbar in Los Angeles, but he also spent part of his college career on a team with legendary shooting guard Michael Jordan at the University of North Carolina.

9. Several forwards have played an entire career of at least 10 years for the Lakers without ever starting a game for another NBA franchise. Vern Mikkelsen was the first to do this. Michael Cooper and James Worthy both lasted for 12 seasons with Los Angeles. Elgin Baylor was the most loyal

among the forwards, spending 14 years with the Lakers and never playing elsewhere.

10. Lakers forward A.C. Green missed only three games during his NBA career and once had an ironman streak of 1,192 consecutive games played. Even the streak was not ended by injury, but rather by Green's retirement in 2001.

CHAPTER 11:

COACHES, GMS, & OWNERS

QUIZ TIME!

1. Who served as the Lakers' first general manager?

    a. John Kundla

    b. George Mikan

    c. Max Winter

    d. Bill Sharman

2. Lakers coach Phil Jackson has authored eight books, including three specifically about his time coaching Los Angeles during the 2000s.

    a. True

    b. False

3. The Lakers' first head coach, John Kundla, lasted for how long in that position?

    a. 82 games

    b. 206 games

    c. 444 games

    d. 725 games

4. The Lakers' most recent coach, Frank Vogel, spent time in coaching positions with each of the following NBA franchises except for which one?

   a. San Antonio Spurs
   b. Boston Celtics
   c. Indiana Pacers
   d. Orlando Magic

5. Who has owned the Minneapolis/Los Angeles Lakers for the longest time?

   a. Jack Kent Cooke
   b. Bob Short
   c. Dr. Jerry Buss
   d. Ben Berger

6. Of all the Los Angeles bench bosses who have coached over 100 NBA games with the team, which one had the lowest regular-season winning percentage at only 0.227?

   a. Byron Scott
   b. Luke Walton
   c. Mike D'Antoni
   d. Joe Mullaney

7. Los Angeles is the only NBA franchise to have a player rise from playing for the team to ownership of the team.

   a. True
   b. False

8. Which coach led the Lakers to their first NBA championship?

a. Pat Riley

b. Del Harris

c. John Kundla

d. Fred Schaus

9. Which of the following Lakers general managers was NOT a player on the team before getting the chance to guide it from the front office?

a. George Mikan

b. Jerry West

c. Magic Johnson

d. Rob Pelinka

10. Who is the franchise leader in coaching wins?

a. Pat Riley

b. Del Harris

c. John Kundla

d. Phil Jackson

11. Which of the following professional sports teams was NOT owned by Lakers owner Jack Kent Cooke?

a. Los Angeles Kings of the National Hockey League

b. Toronto Blue Jays of Major League Baseball

c. Los Angeles Wolves of the North American Soccer League

d. Washington Redskins of the National Football League

12. Twelve people have had an ownership stake in the Lakers over the course of franchise history.

a. True

b. False

13. How many of the Lakers' 24 head coaches have spent their entire NBA coaching careers with the franchise?

    a. 8
    b. 13
    c. 17
    d. 20

14. Which Lakers general manager has led the franchise to the most playoff appearances?

    a. Jerry West
    b. Louis Mohs
    c. Mitch Kupchak
    d. Max Winter

15. In eight seasons coaching the Lakers, how many times did Pat Riley finish above .500 AND win the division title?

    a. 3
    b. 5
    c. 6
    d. 8

16. Pat Riley was honored with the Chuck Daly Lifetime Achievement Award by his peers in the NBA Coaches Association in 2012.

    a. True
    b. False

17. How did Jim Buss become part-owner of the Lakers in 2014?

    a. He purchased the team when the previous owners wished to sell.

b. He inherited a portion of the team from his father.

c. He forced a takeover of the corporation that had previously owned the team.

d. He was hired as CEO of the company that owned the team.

18. Which Los Angeles Lakers owner is a member of the Canadian Baseball Hall of Fame?

a. Jerry Buss
b. Jack Kent Cooke
c. Bob Short
d. Magic Johnson

19. Which of the following Lakers coaches is the only one NOT to have won the Red Auerbach Trophy as NBA Coach of the Year, while behind the bench for Los Angeles?

a. Del Harris
b. Pat Riley
c. Bill Sharman
d. Phil Jackson

20. Lakers owner Jack Kent Cooke once proposed trading franchises with New York Yankees owner George Steinbrenner as part of a business deal.

a. True
b. False

QUIZ ANSWERS

1. C – Max Winter

2. A – True

3. D – 725 games

4. A – San Antonio Spurs

5. C – Dr. Jerry Buss

6. A – Byron Scott

7. B – False

8. C – John Kundla

9. D – Rob Pelinka

10. D – Phil Jackson

11. B – Toronto Blue Jays of Major League Baseball

12. A – True

13. A – 8

14. C – Mitch Kupchak

15. D – 8

16. A – True

17. B – He inherited a portion of the team from his father.

18. B – Jack Kent Cooke

19. D – Phil Jackson

20. B – False

DID YOU KNOW?

1. In the team's early years, center George Mikan bought one-third of the Laker's ownership stake. He sold that share two years later, but when the team faced the prospect of moving to Los Angeles, Mikan actually proposed mortgaging his home to re-purchase the club and keep it in Minneapolis.

2. Five men have served as both coach and general manager of the Lakers. Four of them were behind the bench first (John Kundla, Fred Schaus, Bill Sharman, and Jerry West), while George Mikan ran the team as GM and stepped in to coach just briefly for part of one season.

3. In addition to the Lakers and other sports franchises, Los Angeles owner Jack Kent Cooke also owned the Chrysler Building in New York City, the Los Angeles *Daily News*, and Cablevision.

4. As a Lakers bench boss, Fred Schaus took the team to the NBA Finals four times in the 1960s and lost all four. Schaus finally reached the promised land after moving to the general manager position, when he helped lead Los Angeles to the 1972 NBA championship.

5. Los Angeles owner Jerry Buss was not just referred to as "Dr. Jerry Buss" for fun. He actually holds Master of Science and PhD degrees in physical chemistry from the University of Southern California. Buss worked as a

chemist for the government, contributed his time to the aerospace industry, and then became a faculty member at his alma mater in the chemistry department.

6. Relatively few top NBA executives are born outside of the United States. The very first general manager of the Lakers, Max Winter, was one. Winter was born in 1903 in Austria-Hungary and guided the team for six successful seasons as GM, from 1947-48 through 1953-54.

7. Lakers coach Butch van Breda Kolff resigned his position with the team after a difficult playoff loss in 1969. Van Breda Kolff had openly feuded with the team's superstar center, Wilt Chamberlain, and refused to play Chamberlain at the end of Game 7 of the NBA Finals, which the Lakers lost to the Boston Celtics by just two points.

8. Current Lakers coach Frank Vogel appeared in a segment called "Stupid Human Tricks" on the *Late Show with David Letterman* as a child. Even then, he was focused on basketball and demonstrated his ability to twirl the ball on a toothbrush as he brushed his teeth.

9. Lakers owner Jack Kent Cooke won an NBA championship in 1972 with the Lakers. But he was more successful in football, where he won three Super Bowl victories as the owner of the Washington Redskins

10. Despite 17 NBA titles for the franchise, only one Lakers general manager has been awarded the NBA Executive of the Year Award. Jerry West received the honor in 1994-95,

a year in which Los Angeles finished third in its division and fifth in its conference, and lost in the second round of the playoffs.

CHAPTER 12:

THE AWARDS SECTION

QUIZ TIME!

1. Which two Lakers are tied for the most Maurice Podoloff Trophies as league MVP while playing for Los Angeles?

   a. Center Shaquille O'Neal and guard Kobe Bryant
   b. Center Wilt Chamberlain and guard Jerry West
   c. Center Kareem Abdul-Jabbar and guard Magic Johnson
   d. Center Vlade Divac and guard Derek Fisher

2. 'The first Laker to win any major award given out by the NBA was franchise forward Elgin Baylor.

   a. True
   b. False

3. The Lakers have won 17 NBA titles. They won most of those when the trophy went by which name?

   a. NBA Finals Trophy
   b. Walter A. Brown Trophy
   c. Larry O'Brien Trophy

d. A tie between NBA Finals Trophy and Walter A. Brown Trophy

4. In 1996, the NBA announced its 50 Greatest Players in NBA History. How many of these players suited up for the Lakers?

    a. 3
    b. 6
    c. 9
    d. 12

5. The J. Walter Kennedy Trophy, given to an NBA player who shows "great service and dedication to the community," has been awarded to four Lakers players. Which one of the following players did NOT win this award?

    a. Forward Ron Artest
    b. Guard Magic Johnson
    c. Center Pau Gasol
    d. Forward Elgin Baylor

6. How many Lakers have won the Twyman-Stokes Trophy as NBA Teammate of the Year for "selfless play and commitment and dedication to his team"?

    a. 0
    b. 1
    c. 3
    d. 6

7. When *Sports Illustrated* named its NBA All-Decade Team for the 2000s, it included three Los Angeles Lakers: guard Kobe Bryant, center Shaquille O'Neal, and coach Phil Jackson.

   a. True
   b. False

8. Who was the Laker who most recently made the NBA All-Rookie First Team?

   a. Guard Jordan Clarkson
   b. Forward Brandon Ingram
   c. Guard Lonzo Ball
   d. Forward Kyle Kuzma

9. Which Lakers player has taken home four NBA All-Star Game MVP Awards (tied for the most in NBA history)?

   a. Guard Magic Johnson
   b. Guard Kobe Bryant
   c. Guard Jerry West
   d. Center George Mikan

10. Which of these Lakers icons is the only one NOT to lead the NBA in scoring?

   a. Center George Mikan
   b. Guard Kobe Bryant
   c. Center Shaquille O'Neal
   d. Guard Magic Johnson

11. The NBA Sixth Man of the Year Award for best performing player as a substitute has been won only once by a Laker. Who was it?

a. Center Vlade Divac

b. Guard Eddie Jones

c. Forward Lamar Odom

d. Guard Michael Cooper

12. Lakers forward A.C. Green won the Energizer Ironman of the Year Award for his durability and consecutive games streak in 1988.

a. True

b. False

13. Which of the following players is the only player in Lakers history to win the Eddie Gottlieb Trophy as the league's top rookie?

a. Guard Kobe Bryant

b. Guard Magic Johnson

c. Forward Brandon Ingram

d. Forward Elgin Baylor

14. Of the Lakers in the Basketball Hall of Fame, center George Mikan and forward Jim Pollard are the first to play for the franchise. What year did they begin playing with the team?

a. 1945

b. 1948

c. 1960

d. 1966

15. Which Lakers player has been selected for the most career NBA All-Star Games?

a. Guard Kobe Bryant

b. Center Kareem Abdul-Jabbar

c. Center Shaquille O'Neal

d. Forward LeBron James

16. *Sports Illustrated*'s end of decade poll named the Los Angeles Lakers the "franchise of the decade" for the 2000s across all major sports.

a. True

b. False

17. Which Lakers have won the Three-Point Shootout contest held annually at the NBA's All-Star Weekend?

a. Guards Eddie Jones and Kobe Bryant

b. Guard Robert Horry

c. No Laker has won this event.

d. Guards Nick Van Exel, Derek Fisher, and Kobe Bryant

18. Who was the Los Angeles player most recently named to the NBA All-Defensive Team?

a. Center Anthony Davis

b. Guard Kobe Bryant

c. Forward A.C. Green

d. Center Shaquille O'Neal

19. In which years did Los Angeles host the NBA's annual All-Star Game?

a. 1972, 1986, and 1999

b. 1960, 1981, 1995, 2007, and 2016

c. 1980, 2000, and 2020

d. 1963, 1972, 1983, 2004, 2011, and 2018

20. For almost two decades, computer company IBM gave an award to the NBA player judged by its programming formulas to be most valuable to his team. Guard Magic Johnson received the very first award for Los Angeles and center Shaquille O'Neal won it twice consecutively before the award was discontinued.

   a. True
   b. False

QUIZ ANSWERS

1. C – Center Kareem Abdul-Jabbar and guard Magic Johnson

2. B – False

3. C – Larry O'Brien Trophy

4. C – 9

5. D – Forward Elgin Baylor

6. A – 0

7. A – True

8. D – Forward Kyle Kuzma

9. B – Guard Kobe Bryant

10. D – Guard Magic Johnson

11. C – Forward Lamar Odom

12. B – False

13. D – Forward Elgin Baylor

14. B – 1948

15. B – Center Kareem Abdul-Jabbar

16. A – True

17. C – No Laker has won this event.

18. A – Center Anthony Davis

19. D – 1963, 1972, 1983, 2004, 2011, and 2018

20. A – True

DID YOU KNOW?

1. The Joe Dumars Trophy for sportsmanship, ethical behavior, fair play, and integrity was created by the NBA for the 1995-96 season. In the 25 years of its existence, no Laker has ever won this trophy.

2. Each year, the NBA selects three teams of All-NBA players, and the Lakers have been well represented. Of the top eight players with the most career selections, five were chosen while with the Lakers (LeBron James, Kobe Bryant, Kareem Abdul-Jabbar, Shaquille O'Neal, and Jerry West). Karl Malone is also in the top eight, but none of those selections came during his time in Los Angeles.

3. Only four players have earned the NBA's relatively new Lifetime Achievement Award. Despite the low odds, the Lakers are represented in this small category by superstar guard Magic Johnson, who was given the honor in 2018-19.

4. When the NBA announced the top 10 teams in its history in 1996, two versions of the Lakers were selected. The 1971-72 edition of the squad made the cut, with its .841 winning percentage the second highest on the list. The 1986-87 Lakers also got the nod.

5. The Lakers' "Showtime" brand may have been built around flashy offense, but swingman Michael Cooper won the team's only NBA Defensive Player of the Year Award during that era, earning the nod in 1986-87.

6. Los Angeles tends to favor veteran lineups, which is why it may not be surprising that the franchise has rarely won any NBA Rookie of the Month Awards. The Lakers had none at the turn of the century. At that point, the NBA split the award into Eastern and Western conferences, but even with the increased odds, only two Lakers have been so honored this way: Jordan Clarkson in March 2015 and Kyle Kuzma in November 2017.

7. No Minneapolis or Los Angeles Laker has ever won the NBA's Most Improved Player Award.

8. Thanks to their many championships, the Lakers have produced many Bill Russell Trophy winners as the Most Valuable Player in the NBA Finals. This award has been won by guards Jerry West, Magic Johnson, and Kobe Bryant; forwards James Worthy and LeBron James; and centers Wilt Chamberlain, Kareem Abdul-Jabbar, and Shaquille O'Neal. West is the only player to win this award while playing for the losing team.

9. The Lakers have had one winner of the NBA All-Star Weekend Slam Dunk Contest. Kobe Bryant took home the title in 1997 as an NBA rookie.

10. When the NBA celebrated its 50th anniversary by taking a poll to select the top 10 coaches in NBA history, three Lakers coaches made the cut. Phil Jackson won 11 titles (including five with the Lakers), John Kundla took home all five of his titles with the Lakers, and Pat Riley also had five titles, four of which came with the Lakers.

CONCLUSION

There you have it: an amazing collection of Lakers trivia, information, and statistics at your fingertips! Regardless of how you fared on the quizzes, we hope that you found this book entertaining, enlightening, and educational.

Ideally, you knew many of these details but also learned a good deal more about the history of the Los Angeles Lakers, their players, coaches, management, and some of the quirky stories surrounding the team. If you got a little peek into the colorful details that make being a fan so much more enjoyable, then mission accomplished!

The good news is the trivia doesn't have to stop there! Spread the word. Challenge your fellow Lakers fans to see if they can do any better. Share some of the stories with the next generation to help them become Los Angeles supporters too.

If you are a big enough Lakers fan, consider creating your own quiz with some of the details you know that weren't presented here, and then test your friends to see if they can match your knowledge.

The Lakers are a storied franchise. From Minneapolis to Los

Angeles, they have a long history with multiple periods of success and a few that were less than successful. They've had glorious superstars, iconic moments, hilarious tales...but, most of all, they have wonderful, passionate fans. Thank you for being one of them.

www.ingramcontent.com/pod-product-compliance
Lightning Source LLC
Chambersburg PA
CBHW060241030426

42335CB00014B/1564